Thoughts of Mrs Ojo

Foreword By Evang Mike Bamiloye

Thoughts of Mrs Ojo

(A collection of poems on Life, love and faith)

Timi Ojo

AuthorHouse™
1663 Liberty Drive
Bloomington, IN 47403
www.authorhouse.com
Phone: 1-800-839-8640

Published by AuthorHouse   03/22/2012

ISBN: 978-1-4567-8488-1 (sc)
ISBN: 978-1-4567-8489-8 (e)

This book is printed on acid-free paper.

Contents

Dedication & Dates

A Nuisance
To My Lord Jesus Christ, 20ᵗʰ Oct 2009

Upon Death
Sept 2009

Amidst The Fall
Oct 2009

A Lonely Fee
7ᵗʰ Oct 2009

Corollary of a Corrupt Nation
6ᵗʰ Nov 2009

The Captain & I
To, My husband, Joshua. A. Ojo, June 2004

Youe Smile
To, My husband, Joshua. A. Ojo, June 2004

Life's Winter Season, 2004

Time and Chance
27ᵗʰ Oct 2009

What Really is a big Deal
27ᵗʰ Oct 2009

A New Decade
19ᵗʰ Feb 2009

A note to Thabo
19ᵗʰ Feb 2009

Love for the Hateful
11ᵗʰ Sept 2001

A Ring's Story
19ᵗʰ Feb 2009

Greedy Gypsy Lady
Dedicated to the resilient heartbreaker
and the resilient comeback heart broken, 26th Dec 2010

Fame and Fortune
26th Dec 2010

A Deceived deceiver
26th Dec 2010

Still ! . . . . Ticking clocks
26th Dec 2010

Timelessly
29th Dec 2010

A mother's task?
31st Dec 2010

If I were to make like God
31st Dec 2010

A cake I must bake
31 Dec 2010

Not for My worth
In gratitude to my Lord Jesus Christ
28th Sep 2009

Acknowledgements

Throughout the period it took to write this book, and indeed even way before, my life has been greatly influenced by that of my husband's Joshua A.Ojo. Therefore, I'd like to thank him as he has been an immense source of inspiration to me, I love you, thank you so much. I also want to acknowledge and appreciate my father, Dr P.J. Kagbala, thank you Dad for your fatherly support. Am grateful.

I will like to acknowledge and extend my heartfelt gratitude to all my siblings, especially Nathaniel Igbanoi and Loretta as well as their families who by being part of mine holds an inimitable source of delight for which am grateful both to God and them, thank you.

My sincere thanks also goes to a couple I greatly admire and appreciate, whose lifestyle and faith has greatly helped to form mine particularly in the past 12 years of my life, thank you Dr Olu & Mrs Gloria Olumide, Lead Pastors of the State's Provinces of The Redeemed Christian Church of God, Delta State, Nigeria. Even during the course of writing this book, Mrs Olumide kindly helped me get out of a dead end in order to meet my deadline, I want to specially thank you both as you live a life that is so so worthy of emulation, thank you.

I want to particularly thank, Evang. Mike Bamiloye who took out time to go through the manuscript and write the foreword for this book, am grateful. Sir. Finally my thanks goes to Dr Nicholas & Mrs Shola. Ikhu-Omoregbe, Dr Omorege had earlier encouraged my writing even though it was for my academic publications. Thank you Sir. To the rest of my family and friends am very grateful for your kindness and love, God bless and Keep us all to the day of the arrival of His Dear Son, Jesus Christ, Amen.

Timi Ojo

ForeWord

The book Thoughts of Mrs. Ojo provides poems that are unique, simple and entertaining, making poetry reading an interesting undertaking that teens, adults and the elderly will find very attention-grabbing. Timi Ojo writes poems that are kitted with humor and astuteness which are certainly guaranteed to amuse the reader yet inspire them because of their very powerful message on life's intricate issues.

A fervent celebration of a collection of poems, the author analysis themes with which she persuades us to be acquainted with her outlook which are boldly fashioned by the convictions of her faith. Her enthusiasm will fascinate the reader to see life issues from a lighter mood and then from a stronger elucidation. And, interestingly, inside this collection of poems are many hidden truths about spiritual life that touch man's social, physical and marital concerns. Different ranges of people are addressed, advised, counseled and warned. In overall, there are many life's lessons that can make one's heart think more about God and important spiritual issues.

In my own journey of nearly 3 decades as an author and producer of over 40 Christian drama and films I have been inspired to write and make movies that ardently affects man's sojourn on earth and create a thirst for God and I recognize that this book Thoughts of Mrs Ojo is a product of that same inspiration and I find her poems in their simplicity compellingly interesting and I know that any other reader whether of stories or poems will find it captivating as well.

Wishing you Happy reading now and believing we are to expect more of such delightful writings from the Author.

Evang. Mike Bamiloye
Executive Director,
Mount Zion Film Productions, Nigeria.

Lessons on life,
love & faith

A Nuisance?

A complete nuisance
Yet you took me in
In you eyes I see the glee
Bright shinning love
Unmasked, brilliantly clear
That though called a nuisance
In that very instance
I truly believed
You are the substance
In me

Upon Death

Even upon death, everything means nothing
Is just like another that passes
One is mourned upon a terseness
Certainly the other just the same
There isn't much difference
Only that it may be a likely reference
That upon a certain time
Such and such passed thru this way
Nothing is even much worth even in those moments
Certainly everything is even less worth beneath gravity
Just before reaching forth
in the passage of descent or ascent
after one is brought before Him
certainly then and then one will know all that it was worth
for all the time that was given
whether it was for glory or shame

Amidst the fall

He fell off the bike
Not an unusual scenario in Lagos
The bike rider was a reckless one
At the dawn of another day
He was such of many others
That will have it that way
Putting their passengers in jeopardy
Good to say
That his was only a spring
Then many Mr sympathy came along
And for close to an hour
And they talked about what a fall it was
An amusing pastime
well accustomed to the traffic that slowly moved along
In the midst of their consolation
He did not know
that his wallet was gone

A lonely fee

The little left of my social life
Has frizzled away
Vapourizing, thinly away
I look on, in resignation
I am struck with awe
No more parties, no more fun fare
My friends have bade me fare ware
As much as I tried
Is still Just me
I learn to listen to me
My thoughts I share with me
My tears have dried
Those I also used to share with me
Now am left with me listening to me
Maybe this is just a fee
For my self discovery

Corollary of a corrupt nation

A nation, bankrupt of morality
Robbed and ravaged by immorality
Championing corruption
Stripped naked by dishonesty
Burdened with the tenures of theft
In the fallacy of democracy
Of same yoking fellows
so called leaders
Suffering endorsed by a reckless and wicked few
Inflicted by the stabs of insatiable gluttony
Renowned for its medals of shabbiness and gloom
docility termed a happiest people's smile
plugging slowly into despair
left on its own to redeem itself
For even God can do nothing
While good men
Stand and stare
For only men willing to be redeemed
Get redemption

The Captain & I

Take me seriously please
Beneath this supple curve and ebullient skin
Lies a person not only for the sheets, not just for a tease
Made for reason and wisdom
So take me seriously please

This sleek band that sits silently on my finger
Is reminiscent
Of vows spoken, irreversible till eternity
so take me seriously please
This boat is for you and me
True and true
A Captain for the boat
And never two
Yet a Captain without a crew
Is not true
Sink or float
I remain yours
Yet with a team like ours
We can only but win.

Your Smile

The smile you give
Sing to me a song
its rhythm
In consonance with my heartbeat
The smile you give
Takes me a mile further
Every smile a tale
Of the love within
Words spoken through the smile
All truth not delusion
Cradles me with warmth in a cold night
Assurance that tomorrow will be even brighter
Oh these smiles you give!
My shiny armoured knight

Life's Winter Season

Life's winter is but a season
If her feet abides to tarry
Query not her reason
Steer eyes and heart solitarily
Upon the beauty of her comely bossom
Only crest your heart
With faith, for nothing shall be lost
Since fate always hath a summer

Time & Chance

Time and chance happens to them all
Use your time well
For perhaps your chance
Men may by chance take
Then your time is the only chance which men
Can never take
For if by chance your chance is taken
Then your time
Is all you need
To recover your chance

What Really is a Big Deal ?

It is no big deal
If at the dawn of a new day
There is no assurance of your meal
Since at the dusk of the day the sparrow must have had its
hundredth
That in itself is enough assurance for you
So it is no big deal
Except you make it so

It is no big deal
If your heart is broken and shattered
And it seems beyond the reach of mend
That you never want to live or love again
Even both altogether
If for just a moment you search
You will see in His light
That He made the heart a self healing agent
So is no big deal
Except you make it so

If you a re filled with volcanic wrath
Which shouldn't be in the first place
But if it was so
And words were about to erupt
That will never reverse the hurt
If for just a split second you search
You will see in His light
That a song could still brew
You would just turn and walk away
So is no big deal
Except you make it so

It is no big deal
If you are gripped by fear
Its terror unleashed on you
Dazed by its whispered wicked lies
If for an infinitesimally small fraction of a second
You look the other way
You will see in His light
That His encapsulating love
Can boost you with a bout of courage
So is no big deal
Except you make it so

It is no big deal
If everything seems in array against you
And you think of no other way but to spend your day
Crying with self pity waiting on you
If for just a second
You will see in His light
That you could choose to laugh instead of cry
That you could choose to be grateful
Instead of being regretful
So is no big deal
Except you make it so
Nothing really is a big deal
Except you make it so or think so

A New Decade

My times have been few and some seasons
For this Christmases
I am grateful
My eyes have shed plenty tears
Seasons that I questioned why
Some merely just fears
Other were witnesses
To grief, ephemeral of love
my heart, resisted their scares
Celebration of effusive laughter
Did not cease in these seasons
A select, an aftermath
Of wars and battles
For these too I am grateful
at the threshold of the next decade
I wonder at the vainness of my efforts
I wonder and Whine
Is mine to brand the seasons
a wish in heart, another dance
More accolades
at no battles
a wish in heart

A note to Thabo

Maybe it was because of you, maybe it was because of me
which ever case
Father has left for the mines again
When will we tend to ourselves?
for the man is bent over
and the burden pulls his time nearer by the time
Thabo let's face the world ourselves
Adolescents we are no longer
That father should quench our pangs of hunger
While mother was
They toiled for us like slaves
As Indolent fools ours is to party and dine
His has been the mine

Tomorrow at the break of dawn
I set on my journey
Maybe it was because of you, maybe it was because of me
I have set my mind to face the world
It is my time
If it is only the mine there is
Then it too shall be mine

Love for the Hateful

I hate to hate
But when you are so hateful
It will be hateful not to hate
The likes like you
You don't make me cry
All you inspire is dry
Just like you no luster
No love
It is so easy to hate
The likes like you
But the Holy bible
Restrains me
So it is only okay for me
To hate not to love you

A Ring's Story

My diamond studded ring
Its reflection
An assortment of diverse colors
Each a story to tell
Reminiscent of my wedding day
When I first wore it
A bright mild sunny day
Balloons, confetti variedly textured, variedly tinged
Made it all so gay
Even now as I wear it
It still trills
Voluptuous joy
Elicitation of my most memorable day
Now it glitters blue
Against the light
Then it in another tilt
a different hue
Its lively blue sparks
A recollection of the blue
with sliver striped asoke *
Mother-in law Atiyeki wore
On the arrival of my first bundle of joy
Speedily from the village
She came with a mission
Either to be grieved or to grieve
At that I wasn't ready

Against all odds I had my baby
Despite her rumbling, jeering
Finally my jewel had arrived
With bright beryl eyes
Reflection of his father's
Tiny fingers, that curled in ecstasy
As his mouth tugged in his feeding
Eyes opening occasionally at her bantering
a distraction he couldn't work out
never altering his pleasure
was all my treasure
like soaking away all the pressure
Speedily she had come
At the news of my delivery
Grievously disappointed for her pride
would not allow her to mellow
instead she choose the path of war
she muttered, splattered, sprawling everywhere
with spiteful words
implicitly hurled at me
her swords
I prayed for her to sheath

For when our eyes met
I saw beyond her façade
That she yeaned to hold her grandson
In the agony of her pride
She had lost all discretion
To see that the war was over
Fortunately my hubby

17

Had just gone to the rig
So I had no care

When I had my full
And could take no further
I took to flight and sought refuge in Adago's house
Whose counsel, I only sought after I had decided
Robustly bosomed
Rightly appropriate to her loud mouth

Her words spat fire
Go back give it to her in own her measure
She can't continue to bully you
The baby has come
If only I was her daughter-in law
No, my mind was made
I'll hide here till Aityeki's fiery temper of jealously is
doused
And when she was done and gone
I came quietly back home
To nurture my son and hubby

* Asoke a western Nigerian traditional attire. Names and characters in this
poem are fictious

A Suitor's Dirge

A damsel thou hart
Voluptuous beauty unrivaled
Never in doubt
Like a well crafted sculpture
Very very deeply hollowed
As others not as sought
Grasp in anxiety
Seeking to be desired
Thou more overly sought
Deny to marry
Selfishly in love with thyself
Wanting nothing more but to be by thyself
As others left in great worry
They join all to ponder
Why you choose not to hurry
Oh damsel remember now in thy youth
That beauty presents no anxiety
Yet as more years are bought
Age fades fast away the finest of the finest

Two fools

My virginity
I stole away, to give away, ridiculously free
To a fool
In the name of love
Now I see
blind love
Infatuation
a very costly joke
If I had felt less
Thought more
It would have never been

In foresight
I see the loss
Given for passions of lust
All in a clever façade called love
The only recovery is never to
Remember what a fool
I once was

Lessons on life & love

You & Your Choice

Your choices are you
Your reflections prove your choices
Your paths are your choices
Your choices are your path
Inseparable as can be
Never different from what we see
A sum total of what you are
A summary of what you shall be

As cultured as can be
It is only you to choose
If vile, if kind none else to blame but self
Daily you choose the paths to cross
Not father nor mother
Very well schooled and taught ?
Yet you alone are to choose
Never another
You alone none else to blame none else to glory

Love like Hate

The violin strings
Twine, tightly tied
Total helplessness harping here harping there
Down and up,
Down and up
Yielding to the harping bow
Melody and melody made
Endlessly it gives
Hoping each pitch
Becomes the ending note
Wanting more and more music played
Not wanting to be strung

My Mummy

I loved you dearly
Daily I wanted to call
And when I did
Whether sad or happy
I loved you dearly
In kind & firm voice
You blessed me
Your strength, a shield from your deep grief
Teaching me the value of being loved
Special you made me feel
Because you were special
I really felt special
I loved you dearly my mummy
I don't miss you
You are here in my heart

Dedicated to the memory of my late mother, Patience Adeyemi Iyekepolor. 19/12/ 10

Allan's fiercest Storm

In August 29th of 1864
Rose the fiercest storm
Ever known to Bristol town
It billowed and raged
sauntering through the cricking Clifton bridge
Was Allan Woodman's wagon
Drenching wet, shivering cold and piercing
very very slowly through
Allan thundered the Storm aren't you scared of me
To flee from my fury and rage
As these others that seek refuge from
my torrential wrath
At this Allan sighed and said I dread no other
Than the vampire wife's storm
With her vile and heinous tongue
For yours is just a teacup of a storm

• The name of character in the poem is fictitious

Only with You

Appetites all by a touch gently stirred
Bacon nor ham in the menu
Chocolate and cream entwined
Desires much like cream
Ecstasy, a releasing reservoir,
Fantasies fulfilled filling like yummy cream
Granted pleasures
Head by head lay
Icily calmed
Jointly savoring these moments
Laying quietly still, staring at the ceiling

Dedicated to the faithful spouse.

Till Sparkling & Pained

Down dripping drips of coal
After a chimney's version next better told
Sponged, bitterly dripping through the drapes of coal
tracks of dirt unfold
None stop till sparkling, a glimmer not enough

Longing of the bleeding pots and pans to die rather in thickened coal
Than bear the stripes of the wife's gripping hold
glittering pots and pans, pride of all heated kitchen And pantry too
palaces, cottages seek same, that such adorn their fold

food in such splendid glory
a lusty desire for all
save kettle and pans who bare their grieving story
giving and giving only to fall
first to the gory fiery fire
then down at the wife's threading sponge again to fall

The Greatest Love

Love me, hate me, none matter most
Than a love for me the most
A love lost can't be found except truly by me
Love of self is the greatest gain
After the love of God a happy truth to know
Soonest embraced less of grief and evil bear
Love thy God love thy neighbor as thyself
A love of me than is greatest after God's

Now it takes its tow

Alone alone and none with me
Bitter but bliss
My butter and cheese none to share
In blistering winter cold
given to drink and pipe
yester years and now
today, here their tow
neither a dime or penny to share
friend, wife, even vilest foe depart
alone alone none with me
bitter but bliss
I alone to bear

How He Glowed

A tidy sum a tidy sum
then the grief in my heart will be gone
if you do a tidy work

all he did was hell
never a boon or spoon he owned
but to beat me blue black, then he glowed

must it be such a bum
I rather be alone
Than marry one that is such a scum

The devil's wipe never felt so bad
I went to hell and back
pay him on his back

Mantaga's lullaby

Forlorn a face set with a million lines
Mantaga sat with ease on her rocking chair
a story to tell of a wealthy heir
Then sing us to sleep Mantaga, a pretty bane

A throaty croak came the first line, a gruffy note
the triplets tossed and shrieked beneath their pane
with a voice like yours the devil will be restive in his Lune
angrily Mantaga gave another rasping note

Oh no Mantaga not another lest we die
miles nearer yours is to the grave we are only yet babes
should we bear these jibes
we seek to bud at the crack of dawn and not to die
at the rumble of your voice
only bid us a melody to sleep

very well Mantaga replied
yours is to listen and then sleep shall call
if you be so insolent and rumpled
the devil your funeral he shall attend with glee as a ball
save you let me now sing you to sleep

An African woman: full figured

African wife a typical model, full bellied
Contoured with wide voluptuous hips
My waist is narrowly shaped
And if I choose
Draping of beautiful beads on its rounded line adorn
Solomon never saw one like these hastily he would have acquired
one his galleries to adorn
If he had only seen one like me

Bathsheba took his fancy
Ah! Side by side a gallant vanquish
She would have been !
If only he had seen one like me

roundly contoured
My hips are wide and vey hippy
My belly like the back of a well rounded palm wine calabash*
And my navel like a berry, a dimple on a well kneaded dough
My husband loves me like a jewel
Solomon too would have taken to my fancy
If he had only seen one like me

* calabash: the hollow shell of a gourd, used as a bowl, cup, etc

Gone too soon

Never been this cold
Never been this sad
Like hot then cold
A mixture of them both

Never leaving the memories of you
Crying every day
Miserable every now and then
Wanting to see you wanting to touch you
But you are gone

Dedicated to the memory of my late mother, Patience Adeyemi Iyekrpolor

Greedy Gypsy Lady

I must try today
To get along, to live and be gay
without you
greedy gypsy lady
seeking only to take my bread
never loving to love
merely grabbing joyful trophies
of broken hearts here and there
Calmly waiting for me
To bow but I shall not!
Place to place you trot
Seeking another to hurt

Dedicated to the resilient heartbreaker and the resilient comeback heart broken

Fame and Fortune

Fame and fortune hand by hand I seek
If am to choose between the two I rather have fortune in bliss
In quiet I will be, to enjoy the monies that will last a life time
For fame often has its gory pain
These are silent and stern
Aching deep within the heart
Never telling another these pain
Though from land to land many can only see its glow.
Fortune though has all gain
If bridled well
Kept from the ashes of hell
A tool for treasures of heavenly bliss
And a price for earthly rest
Again & again give me fortune for if there is only it to choose
I will gladly take its hand
If well bridled and tamed
The paths of heavenly pearly gates it may lead
Only the love of it takes the downwards paths
So many have had their hearts and souls fixedly bruised
Never giving all the gain
Back in glory to Him who truly owns
Every dust of gold there is to own

Oh Prickling pin

My heart has lost its joy
And a prickling pin pickles it back to life and fervor
It mustn't accustom itself to pain but lend it to the gains of life
Not to whine at the fiercest of tongues
For such at dawn and dusk seek to break
Every fiber of love within
To leave it empty and very dry
Oh prickling pin, oh night I say to thee
Prickle it back to know
Every day must be with night
All that is gay is never true
That in itself makes it gay
Oh prickling pin, oh night I say to thee
Prickle it back to love
to gird with strength and truth
the gains of the lusty lawns and fields of bliss
The sunshine that greets at the break of even dawn
The running waters that give breath to the steeping stream beneath
Bowing in surrender to the valley below
To hear the glee of happy babies' cheers
and be thankful for the nightingale lending voice
sweetly breaking the icy calm
that fills the frosty air and haze
of the early harmattan morning

* harmattan: a dry, dusty wind that blows from the Sahara in N Africa toward the Atlantic, esp. from Nov. to March.

A Deceived deceiver

The leopard of a man sought to lure the blossoming beauty
Like a dove he sang his songs of love
Yet a snake he sought to make
Seeking the budding bosom of her tender embrace
In devouring mind, a hope and feat
Of lofty stately heights to claim
In between her legs he sought to take

His eyes were slit and red
A filling of the local red gin
A prince like me will pay any price for your hand
He said, in his stench of a breath
Is love that brews in every inch of my heart
He forgot that he lost his heart in the brewery house

Left with him was a stomach filled with gin and beer
A mini brewery for all that lot
While he made his plot
She saw that his was only an empty head
For though her years
Were very few she had sat long on the pew
To know what a gutter of a man
He really was.

Still !.... ticking clocks

Hours ending, the clock comes ticking
The day draws nearer to a close, then opens another night
Round and round it goes and never ending it seems to be

And dreams, yet to birth
Mansions yet to earth
Away the clock ticks away
Hurrying in another day
Still be still!
Keep tomorrow at bay
Until am ready and gay

Today must be still
A promise to my bride I have made
Tomorrow do not come, till am certain
The dowry, none yet to pay
Ticking clocks make a pause
And wait a while till am ready

Timelessly

In hell I must tell
Nothing is really well
why most hurry
Seeking to pay his rusty gushing fare
I wonder
Angrily discarding reason
In timeless season they still go
From Herod till now
Restraining from counsel not to sell
Their soul to hell

A mother's task?

From standing and sitting
Stirring at the pudding
Then scrubbing and baking
Then baking and cooking
An aching back is often for the telling
Show of a little love better than any farthing
And a mother shall never complain
For a mother's truest task is to love

A mind Lonely and Idle

The devil will lead you into disarray
Deceitful as can be
A mind will he rewind and unwind
Heaps and heaps to pile
till all that is left, is stench
And when you are all alone and forlorn
A hammer he will soon strike
A mind should never be lent to him

If I were to make like God

If I were to make like God
I will Make myself happy
I will Make my home happy
I will Make my friends happy
I will Make my lover bliss

Cake I must bake

A cake I must bake
A must if am to take
Another bitter pill of dr jake
deep regrets I wish my teeth not to ache
and never so sore for a pill to take
sweets a sore pleasure and never in haste to ask
but a cake I must take

Not for my Worth

Not for my worth
He did purchase
Eternal bliss
For an unjust case
None would come forth
Not even on lease
For many would only cry foul
Love driven by Love
Stripped His matchless worth
And bowed to death
A shameful one at that
In rescue of a lost soul

In gratitude to My Lord, Jesus Christ, 28-09-09

About the Author

Timi Ojo teaches computer science in Lagos state polytechnic, Lagos state, Nigeria and as an armature poet writing simply on life's issues presents her first book, Thoughts of Mrs Ojo. The poems are written from her personal perspective on issues formed mainly by her Christian faith and her life's experience and she writes poems that seek to both enlighten and entertain her readers

Timi Ojo is married to Joshua A. Ojo and lives in Lagos, Nigeria.

Printed in the United States
By Bookmasters